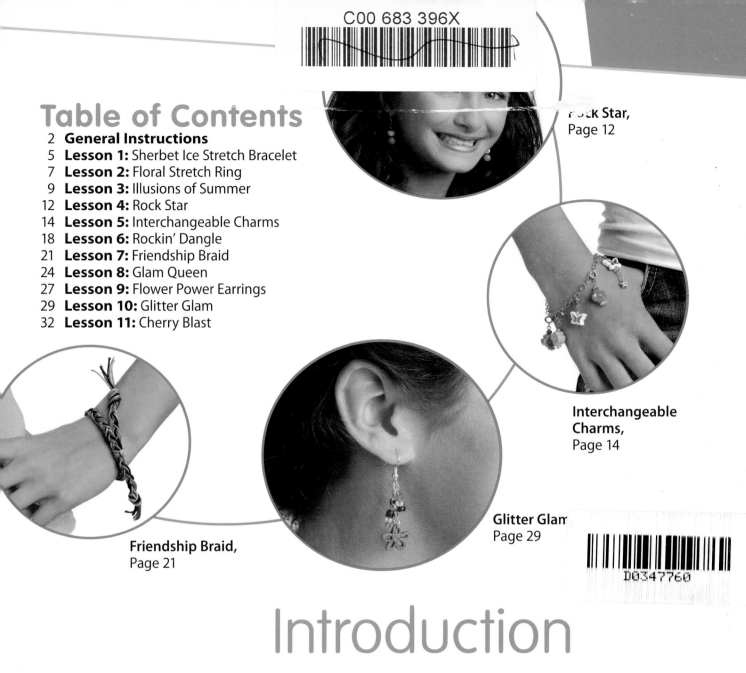

Table of Contents

Rock Star,
Page 12

Interchangeable Charms,
Page 14

Friendship Braid,
Page 21

Glitter Glam
Page 29

Introduction

Creating your own jewelry is easy and fun. You can choose bead colors and shapes to suit your individual style. You'll love the compliments you get when wearing jewelry you designed. In this book you will learn different techniques to make bracelets, necklaces, earrings, headbands and dangles. We'll give you ideas on beads to use for each project. You may not be able to find the same beads we used, but that's OK. You make the jewelry distinctly yours by selecting beads you like best. Use these lessons over and over to create different looks just by changing the beads.

Annie's™ *I Can Bead* is published by Annie's, 306 East Parr Road, Berne, IN 46711. Printed in USA. Copyright © 2012 Annie's. All rights reserved. This publication may not be reproduced in part or in whole without written permission from the publisher.
RETAIL STORES: If you would like to carry this pattern book or any other Annie's publication, visit AnniesWSL.com
Every effort has been made to ensure that the instructions in this pattern book are complete and accurate. We cannot, however, take responsibility for human error, typographical mistakes or variations in individual work. Please visit AnniesCustomerCare.com to check for pattern updates.
ISBN: 978-1-59635-562-0
123456789

General Instructions

Use the information in this section to help you select the correct sized beads, findings and tools to complete your projects.

BEADS
Bead Size Chart

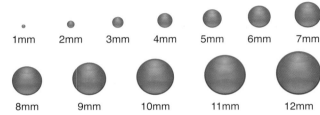

1mm 2mm 3mm 4mm 5mm 6mm 7mm

8mm 9mm 10mm 11mm 12mm

Bead Shapes

Beads come in a wide variety of shapes. Below are a few of the common shapes.

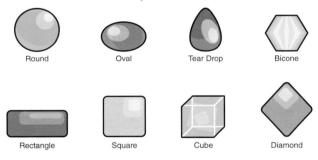

Round   Oval   Tear Drop   Bicone

Rectangle   Square   Cube   Diamond

STRINGING MATERIALS

You can use many different materials to string your beads. Each lesson will note which material is used for stringing. When choosing stringing material, always make sure it will fit through the holes in your beads.

Flexible Beading Wire is made from flexible strands of wire twisted together. It comes in various sizes and colors.

Cord comes in satin, leather, suede, hemp, rayon and cotton. It is available in various sizes and colors and is great to use when you want to add knots to your design.

Elastic is used for making quick and easy bracelets and rings. Make sure the thickness of the elastic will go through the beads you are using.

Ribbon comes in a variety of sizes and colors. It is great for adding texture to your designs. Make sure the ribbon will go through the hole in your beads.

JEWELRY FINDINGS

Jewelry findings come in a variety of colors. Try to match the color of all your findings as closely as possible for each jewelry project.

Chain is available in small to large links.

Clasps are the ends of your bracelet or necklace project that hold it together. There are many styles. The most common are shown below.

Hook-and-eye   Lobster-claw   Barrel

Spring-ring

Bar-and-ring toggle

Crimp Beads and Tubes are used at the beginning and ends of your beading wire to hold your clasp. They can also be used with beads to make them appear to float on the wire.

Earring Findings come in many colors and styles. Pick the right style for you.

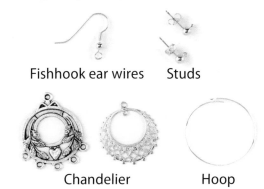

Fishhook ear wires   Studs

Chandelier   Hoop

Eye Pins are a straight pin with a loop on one end.

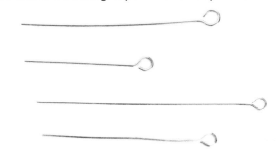

Head Pins are a straight pin with a flattened end.

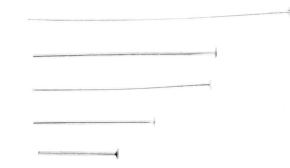

Jump Rings come in many sizes and colors and are used to hold your jewelry together and to create designs.

Split Rings are not just for key chains. They can be used in jewelry designs too.

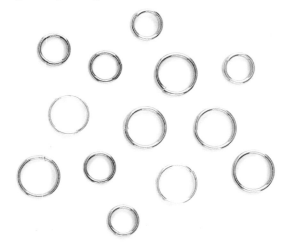

TOOLS

Beading Mats or Bead Design Boards help you lay out your design and keep your beads from rolling away.

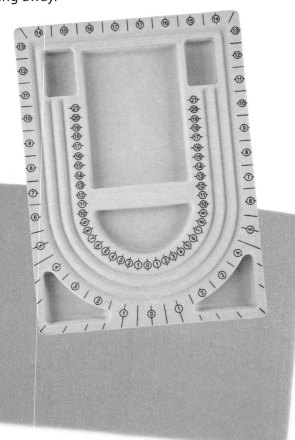

Chain-Nose Pliers are flat on the inside and have a small pointed end. They can be used to work in small places and to help open jump rings.

Crimp Pliers are used to close and fold crimp beads and tubes.

Round-Nose Pliers are used to create loops and curves in wire.

Side-Cutting Pliers are used to cut wire, chain, rings, pins and more. ●

Lesson 1
Sherbet Ice Stretch Bracelet

Design by **Sharon Frank**

String this sherbet-colored bracelet in your favorite colors. Wear it alone or create multiple bracelets to swap with friends for a different look each day.

YOU WILL NEED:

- 9 (8mm) coordinating orange and yellow beads in solid and stripes
- 3 (10mm x 12mm) green oval beads
- 6 (6mm) rondelle beads in coordinating color
- E beads: 10 yellow, 10 green
- Household string or yarn
- 12 inches lime green elastic beading cord
- Scissors
- Ruler
- Household tape
- Jewelry glue or clear-drying craft glue

MAKE YOUR BRACELET:

1. Wrap a piece of string or yarn loosely around your wrist. Remember, beads will make the bracelet tighter, so make sure the string is a little loose around your wrist, but it should not be able to slide off your hand (Figure 1).

2. Cut the string at the length you like. Set aside.

3. Wrap a piece of tape about 1 inch from one end of your green elastic beading cord. This will help keep your beads from falling off the cord while you are stringing.

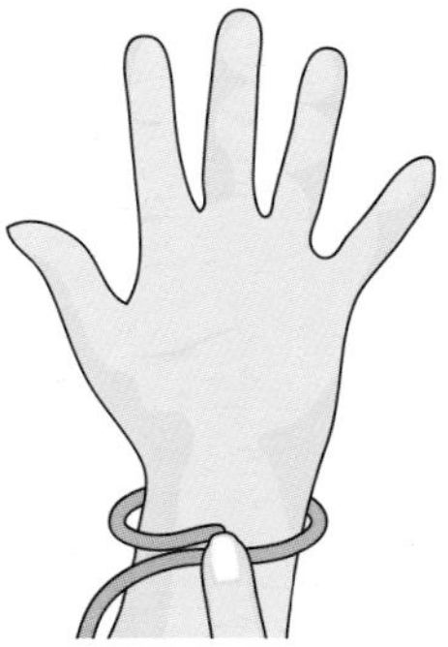

Figure 1

4. Lay your beads out in a row on your mat in the design you like. Don't forget to read the Design Tip. You can lay the beads like our picture, or make your own design. Make the row of beads the same length as the string you wrapped around your wrist (Figure 2).

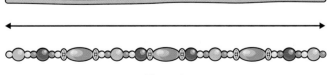

Figure 2

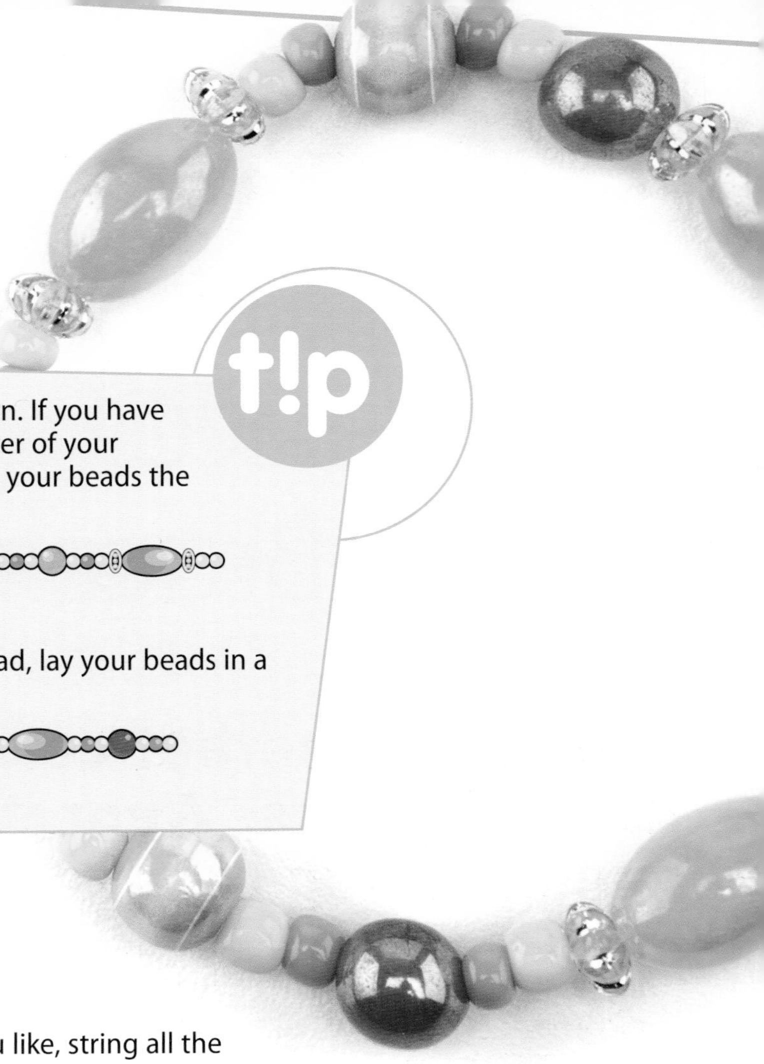

Lay out your beads in a pleasing pattern. If you have one special bead you want for the center of your bracelet, start in the center and lay out your beads the same on each side (Figure 3).

Figure 3

If you are not using a special center bead, lay your beads in a repeating pattern (Figure 4).

Figure 4

t!p

5. When you have the beads laid out in a pattern you like, string all the beads onto the elastic cord (Figure 5).

tape →

Figure 5

6. When all the beads are on the cord, place a piece of tape at the end of the elastic to keep the beads from falling off. Hold the elastic cord together at the ends of the beads and test fit the bracelet on your wrist. You can add beads or take beads off to make it fit just right.

7. Tie a **surgeon's knot** *(see illustration)* in the elastic cord to secure the ends together. Do not cut the extra cord yet.

Surgeon's Knot

8. Let the elastic cord sit for a few minutes. This will allow the elastic to relax. Gently pull the knot tight again to make sure it is very secure. Put a dot of jewelry glue or clear-drying craft glue on the knot. Let dry and trim ends of elastic. ●

Lesson 2
Floral Stretch Ring

Design by **Corene Painter**

This stretch ring is the perfect match for the Sherbet Ice Stretch Bracelet. Keep it for yourself, or give as a great gift!

YOU WILL NEED:
- Coordinating E beads in desired colors
- Coordinating small seed beads
- 6mm rondelle beads in coordinating color
- Small silver metal flower beads
- Large plastic floral focal bead
- Household string or yarn
- 2 (10 inches) elastic beading cord
- Scissors
- Ruler
- Household tape
- Jewelry glue or clear-drying craft glue

MAKE YOUR RING:
1. Wrap a piece of string or yarn loosely around your finger. Beads will make the ring tighter, so make sure the string is a little loose around your finger, but it should not be able to slide off (Figure 1).

2. Cut the string at the length you like. Set aside.

Figure 1

3. Wrap a piece of tape about 1 inch from one end of your elastic beading cord. This will help keep your beads from falling off the cord while you are stringing.

4. Lay your first strand of beads out in a row on your mat in the design you like or following the design in Figure 2. Add seed beads or E beads as needed to the design until your design is the same length as the string or yarn you used to measure your finger (Figure 2).

Figure 2

5. When you have the beads laid out in a pattern you like, place a piece of tape on one end of your elastic cord. This will keep your beads from falling off when stringing. Beginning at one end, string all the beads onto the elastic cord.

6. When all the beads are on the cord, place a piece of tape at the end of the elastic to keep the beads from falling off. Hold the elastic cord together at the ends of the beads and test fit the ring on your finger. You can add seed beads and E beads or take seed beads or E beads off to make it fit just right.

7. Lay another row of beads out on your mat that follow the same pattern you used on the first cord. This time do not add a focal floral bead or a metal floral bead to the pattern, just leave spaces for them (Figure 3).

Figure 3

8. Wrap a piece of tape about 1 inch from one end of your second piece of elastic beading cord.

9. Begin stringing your second pattern of beads onto the elastic cord. When you reach the space for your focal floral bead, thread the cord through the focal floral bead on your first strand of beads (Figure 4).

Figure 4

10. Continue to string the rest of your beads. When you reach the end of your pattern, thread your cord through the metal flower bead on your first strand of beads (Figure 5).

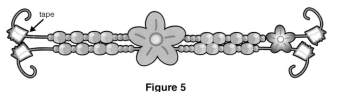

Figure 5

11. Remove the tape from ends of second beaded strand. Tie a **surgeon's knot** *(see illustration)* in the elastic cord to secure the ends together. Do not cut the extra cord yet.

Surgeon's Knot

12. Let the elastic cord set for a few minutes. This will allow the elastic to relax. Gently pull the knot tight again to make sure it is very secure. Put a dot of jewelry glue or clear-drying craft glue on the knot. Let dry and trim ends of elastic.

13. Remove the tape from the ends of your first strand of beads and repeat steps 11–12. ●

t!p

Your focal flower bead may have a large hole. If it does, make sure that the beads you string on either side of the focal floral bead are large enough so they won't slip into the hole.

Make sure your focal floral bead and your metal floral bead have large enough holes in them so your elastic cord will fit through the beads twice.

Lesson 3
Illusions of Summer

Design by **Carrie Walters**

Dreaming of summer? With this necklace it can feel like summer all year long!

YOU WILL NEED
- 48 (4mm) bicone crystal beads: 16 blue, 16 green, 16 yellow
- Peace charm with jump ring
- 56 (2mm) crimp tubes
- 2 (19-inch) 7-strand beading wire (0.018in)
- 2 (8mm) split rings
- 6mm x 9mm lobster-claw clasp
- Crimp pliers
- Flush cutters
- Ruler

MAKE YOUR NECKLACE:

1. Slide your lobster clasp onto a split ring. A split ring is like a key ring, lift up one end with your fingernail and slide lobster clasp on and slide it until it reaches the center of the ring.

2. String crimp tube onto one end of both beading wires approximately 1½ inches from one end. Pass short wire tails through split ring with lobster claw attached and back through the crimp tube. Position crimp tube ¼ inch from split ring (Figure 1).

Figure 1

3. Position crimp in C-shaped (back) hole of crimp pliers. Squeeze gently but firmly to crimp (Figure 2a, Step 1).

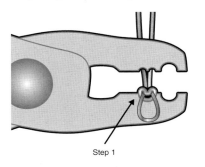

Step 1

Figure 2a

9

4. Turn flattened crimp on its side and position into front hole of crimp pliers. Squeeze gently but firmly to fold crimp tube in half to finish crimping (Figure 2b, Step 2). **Note:** *Gently tug on lobster claw to be sure crimp tube is secure.* Trim short ends of wire with flush cutters next to crimp tube as close as possible.

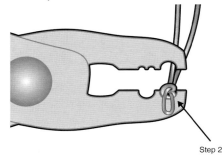

Step 2

Figure 2b

5. Working with wire 1, slide on a crimp tube and crimp 1 inch from crimp holding the split ring (Figure 3).

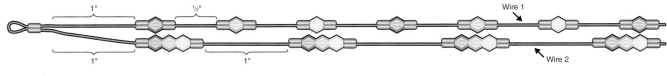

Figure 3

6. String one 4mm bicone crystal bead and a crimp tube. Crimp the crimp tube as close to the 4mm bicone crystal bead as you can. Be careful when crimping, try not to crimp your bicone crystal bead, the bead will break if you do. **Note:** *Refer to Figure 3 and photo for the color pattern to string the crystals in or create your own. Keep in mind that Figure 3 only shows a small section of the necklace.*

7. String another crimp tube ½ inch from the last one and crimp in place.

8. Repeat steps 6 and 7 until you have 18 beads crimped on the wire.

9. Working with wire 2, slide on a crimp tube and crimp 1 inch from crimp holding the split ring (Figure 3).

10. String three 4mm bicone crystal beads and a crimp tube. Crimp the crimp tube as close to the last 4mm bicone crystal bead as you can.

11. String another crimp tube 1 inch from the last one and crimp in place.

12. Repeat steps 10 and 11 three more times.

t!p

When laying out your beads, you can either lay them out in a pattern or lay them out randomly. For example, a pattern will be yellow, green, blue, yellow, green, blue or randomly will be yellow, blue, yellow, blue, green, green.

13. String three 4mm bicone crystal beads, peace charm, three 4mm bicone crystal beads and a crimp tube. Crimp the crimp tube as close to the last 4mm bicone crystal bead as you can (Figure 4).

Figure 4

14. Repeat step 11. Repeat steps 10 and 11 three more times.

15. Repeat step 10 once. ***Note:*** *You should have a total of 8 sets of 3 beads and 1 set of 6 center beads on wire 2.*

16. String crimp tube onto the end of both beading wires approximately 1 inch from the last crimp tubes. Pass short wire tails through remaining split ring and back through the crimp tube. Position crimp tube ¼ inch from split ring and crimp.

17. Trim wire ends close as possible to crimp tube.

18. Open jump ring on peace charm and place wire 1 into jump ring. To open a jump ring hold one side between your thumb and finger and the other side with the round nose pliers. Make sure the opening is facing up. Gently twist the ends sideways to open. Do not pull the ends apart; this will break your jump ring (Figure 5). Once you have added the wire, twist the jump ring closed again. ●

Figure 5

Lesson 4
Rock Star

Design by **Carrie Walters**

Dress it up or rock it out! This headband can be made in any color or style to match your personality.

MAKE YOUR HEADBAND:

1. Leaving a 6-inch tail, start wrapping the long end of wire around the headband approximately 3½ inches from one end of the headband (Figure 1).

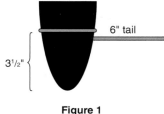

6" tail

3¹/₂"

Figure 1

2. Wrap long end of wire around headband twice, leaving about a ³/₁₆-inch space between the wraps.

3. Slide E beads onto the wire (either in a pattern or randomly) to cover the width of the headband.

4. Repeat step 2 and 3 until you reach the other side of the headband about 3½ inches from the end (Figure 2). **Note:** *You will need to add more beads to your pattern on your wire where the headband is wider.*

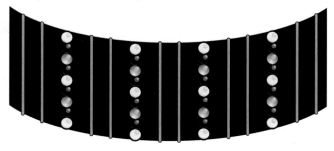

Figure 2

YOU WILL NEED
- Headband
- 2 tubes of 6/0 E beads: 1 clear with silver lining, 1 black opaque
- 10-foot length of 20-gauge silver wire
- Ruler
- Round-nose pliers
- Flush cutters

Use different color beads, wire and headbands to create designer headbands for all your outfits. When using wire, make sure to keep the end of the wire away from your face. The cut edge is very sharp and can scratch or poke you if you are not careful. Please ask an adult for help if you need it.

5. Trim wire to 2½ inches.

6. Use your round-nose pliers to grasp the very end of the wire. Roll the wire until it touches itself. You may have to stop part of the way through to adjust your pliers and complete the roll. The loop will now look like a "b" (Figure 3).

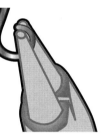

Figure 3

7. Grasp the flat side of the "b" and continue turning to create a spiral (Figure 4).

Figure 4

8. When the spiral is centered in the middle of the headband it is finished. Press spiral flat to headband.

9. Repeat steps 5–9 on other side of headband. ●

Lesson 5

Interchangeable Charms

Design by **Corene Painter**

This layered necklace is fun to make because of the multiple ways you can wear it! Trade your charms with friends or move them around your necklace for a different look!

MAKE YOUR NECKLACE:

1. Open a jump ring and slide on one end of the 6-inch length of chain and a spring ring clasp. To open a jump ring, hold one side between your thumb and finger and the other side with the round-nose pliers. Make sure the opening is facing up. Gently twist the ends sideways to open. Do not pull the ends apart; this will break your jump ring (Figure 1). Once you have added the chain and the clasp, twist the jump ring closed again (Figure 2).

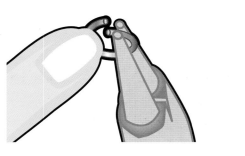

Figure 1

Figure 2

YOU WILL NEED:
- 6/0 seed beads
- Decorative plastic beads in desired colors: flowers, butterflies
- Decorative glass beads in desired colors: rounds, faceted rounds, faceted teardrops (top-drilled), faceted teardrop beads (side-drilled)
- Silver metal flower beads
- Silver metal daisy spacers
- Silver chain: 6-inch length, 16-inch length, 18-inch length, 20-inch length
- 17 (1½-inch) silver head pins
- 6 (1½-inch) silver eye pins
- 4 (6mm) jump rings
- 17 (7mm) spring ring clasps
- Black marker
- Side-cutting pliers
- Round-nose pliers

2. Repeat step 1 on other end of the 6-inch length of chain, creating the back connecting chain (Figure 3).

Figure 3

3. To create a charm, slide desired beads onto a head pin. Push beads down to the bottom of the head pin and place your thumbnail on the top bead on head pin. Bend the head pin over to form an upside-down L shape (Figure 4).

Figure 4

4. Measure about ⅜ inch from the bend and put a mark with a black marker. Use your side-cutting pliers to cut the pin at the mark.

5. To create the simple loop, hold the earring with the tail facing away from you. Grasp end of the head pin in your round-nose pliers, about half way up the nose of the pliers. Roll the pliers toward you to create the loop. Keep rolling until the wire touches itself. You can stop part way through to adjust your pliers and complete the roll (Figure 5).

Figure 5   **Figure 6**

6. Adjust the loop with your pliers until it is in the center of your bead. It should look like a lollipop from the side (Figure 6).

7. Repeat steps 3–6 with remaining 16 head pins and desired beads.

8. Slide desired beads onto an eye pin and form a simple loop. This creates a charm link. Repeat five times for a total of six charm links.

9. Simple loops you make can be opened and closed in the same way as the jump rings are.

Twist open the loops on the charms and connect them to spring ring clasps or bottom loop on charm links. Leave a few charm links without charms connected to them (Figure 7).

Figure 7

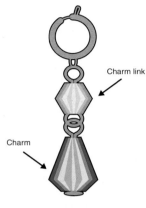

Charm link

Charm

Figure 8

Don't feel like wearing a necklace? That's OK. The back connecting chain of this necklace can be worn as a charm bracelet!

Make sure your chain has large enough links to attach the spring rings.

10. Open top loop of charm link and connect it to spring ring clasps (Figure 8).

11. Open a jump ring and slide a side-drilled teardrop bead and bottom loop of a charm link onto the jump ring. Close Jump ring. Open top loop on charm link and connect to a spring ring clasp (Figure 9). Repeat as desired.

12. Open a spring ring clasp on the back connecting chain and slide ends of 16-inch length, 18-inch length and 20-inch length of chain onto clasp (Figure 10). Repeat with remaining end of the back connecting chain.

Figure 9

Figure 10

13. Connect charms to your necklace in whatever pattern you like! ●

Lesson 6
Rockin' Dangle

Design by **Erica Visocky**

This dangle is rockin' with "rocks" of howlite—a real gemstone—strung on black cord.

MAKE YOUR DANGLE:

1. Gather all of the cords in one hand so that their ends are even. Fold all the cords in half to find the middle. Measure 2½ inches from the middle to one side. Fold a piece of tape around your cord at that line (Figure 1). **Note:** *Figure 1 only shows a small section of the cords.*

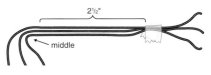

Figure 1

2. Secure your cord to a table with another piece of tape. You can also just clip it into the clipboard.

3. Braid the longer length of cords, as evenly as you can, until you have braided 5 inches. While holding on to the end of your braid, take the cords off your work surface. Pull off the tape from step 1.

4. Tie a big **overhand knot** *(see illustration)* at the bottom of the braid. Make sure that it covers the ends of the braids (Figure 2). **Note:** *If the cords aren't even or flat together, you can pull on the individual cords to pull them into the knot.*

Overhand Knot

Overhand knot

Figure 2

YOU WILL NEED:
- 3 (36-inch) lengths of black 1mm cotton cord
- 3 (4mm) round white howlite beads
- Household tape
- Scissors
- Clipboard (optional)

t!p

Look carefully at the size of holes in your beads. They'll need to fit on one length of cord. You can hold the cord up to the hole to know if the hole is going to work.

Use a clipboard to secure your braid while you knot instead of taping your braid to a table. Using a clipboard makes your braid portable.

5. Secure your cords to a table with tape or onto your clipboard on the big knot or loop.

6. String your beads on one center cord. Tie a knot at the bottom of the cord (Figure 3). Pull your beads back down to the bottom.

7. Create a **flat knot** *(see illustration)* by picking out one outside cord on each side. Cross one over the top of all the cords and the other under all the cords. Push the bottom cord's tail up through the top cord's loop. Push the top cord's tail through the bottom cord's loop. Pull on both tails so that the cords tighten around the center cords and close the loops on either side. You may want to push the cords upward so that they lay next to each other. Finish your flat knot by wrapping the top cord's tail under cords and the bottom cord's tail across the top. Push each tail through the loops and tighten creating a flat knot (Figure 4). Repeat once.

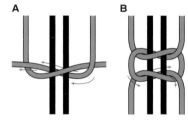

A   B

Flat Knot

Overhand knot

Figure 3

Figure 4

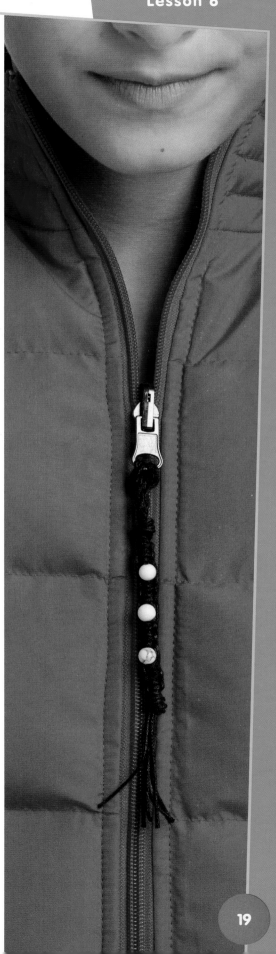

8. Push one bead up against the bottom knot. Create another flat knot underneath the bead. As you tighten your cords, make sure the bead is staying centered. Knot three more flat knots (Figure 5).

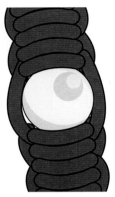

Figure 5

9. Repeat step 8 with your remaining beads.

10. Tie a big overhand knot with all cords at the end of your knotting. Trim the ends as you like.

TO HANG YOUR DANGLE:

1. Pinch the sides of your loop together and thread through the loop of a bag or belt loop (Figure 6). Push the bottom overhand knot of your dangle through the loop of your dangle and pull through (Figure 7). ●

Figure 6

Figure 7

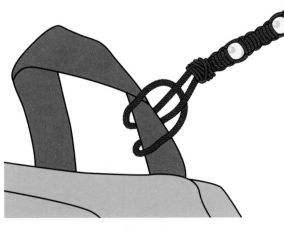

t!p

To make our dangle, we make four knots, add a bead, make four knots and repeat. How do you want all of your beads to look on the dangle? Maybe you want them all together in the center, one at the top, one at the center and one at the bottom. The decision is yours!

Lesson 7
Friendship Braid

Design by **Erica Visocky**

It's easy to make and even easier to adjust to any size! You'll have an armful of bracelets sooner than you think for you and your friends.

MAKE YOUR BRACELET:

1. Wrap a scrap piece of cord loosely around your wrist. Trim the cord where the ends overlap. Use this measurement for your bracelet length (Figure 1).

Figure 1

2. Gather all of the strings in one hand so that their ends are even. Tie an **overhand knot** *(see illustration)* about an inch from the end. Secure your cords on to a work surface with tape or on a clipboard.

Overhand Knot

YOU WILL NEED:
- 2 (24-inch) lengths each of 1mm cotton cord in the following colors: black, red, orange, lime green
- 1 (16-inch) length of lime green 1mm cotton cord
- Household tape
- Scissors
- Clipboard (optional)
- Craft glue (optional)

t!p

Use a clipboard to secure your braid while you knot instead of taping your braid to a table. Using a clipboard makes your braid portable.

3. Split the cords into three sets. You'll have two 3-cord sets and one 2-cord set (Figure 2). Braid the sets as evenly as you can. Braid until you have a length 3 inches longer than your bracelet-length cord. Tie an overhand knot at the bottom of the braids. Trim the ends of the cords to about 1 inch.

Figure 2

t!p

You can change the thickness of this bracelet by adding more cords. Make a thinner one by only using one cord of each color. Not sure what colors you want to use? Look at your favorite band's logo or last album cover and use those colors.

4. Lay the braided ends of the bracelet in opposite directions to create a circle (Figure 3).

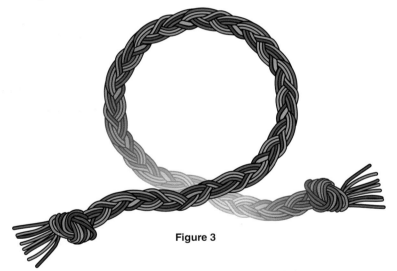

Figure 3

5. Fold one end of your 16-inch lime green cord over itself 5 inches. Lay folded over section of lime green cord on top of overlapping braided ends of bracelet (Figure 4).

Figure 4

6. Wrap long tail of lime green cord around overlapping braided ends of bracelet and folded over 5-inch section of lime green cord six times toward loop (Figure 5).

Figure 5

7. Thread end of cord you were wrapping with through loop. Gently pull short end of lime green cord, closing loop around tail thread through it and pulling it under the wraps (Figure 6). There will now be a lime green cord sticking out both sides of your wrap.

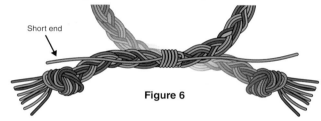

Short end

Figure 6

8. Tie the ends of lime green cord in a double knot. Trim ends close to the knot (Figure 7). ***Note:*** *You can put a little white or craft glue on the knot if you like.*

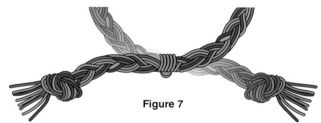

Figure 7

TO WEAR YOUR BRACELET:

1. Pull the sides of the bracelet apart to open it.

2. Slide it on to your wrist. Hold one end of the bracelet with the fingers on the arm wearing it. Use your other hand to pull on the other end (Figure 8). ●

Figure 8

Lesson 8
Glam Queen

Design by **Erica Visocky**

You'll feel like a queen in this glam headband. The best part is it's adjustable so you can share it with your little sister, or maybe not.

MAKE YOUR HEADBAND:

1. Tie one end of each piece of elastic cord to one acrylic jewel or shank button, using a surgeon's knot (Figure 1).

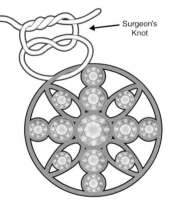

← Surgeon's Knot

Figure 1

> ## t!p
> You can make this headband in any color. Just pick out beads in white, plus light, medium and dark of your favorite colors. Adding clear and frosted beads also adds interest.

2. Thread the needle onto your first elastic cord and string beads according to pattern for strand 1 or using your own pattern (Figure 2). When you're done stringing, remove the needle and tie the end to the other acrylic jewel or shank button, using a surgeon's knot.

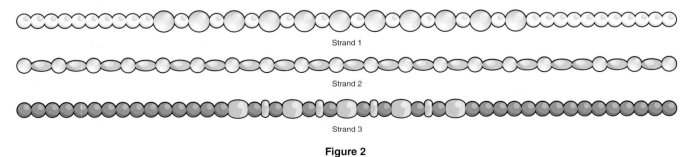

Strand 1

Strand 2

Strand 3

Figure 2

YOU WILL NEED:

- 30 (4mm) round white glass pearls
- 38 (4mm) round dark pink glass pearls
- 18 (5 x 7mm) oval pink glass pearls
- 19 (4mm) round translucent pink glass beads
- 11 (8mm) round translucent pink glass beads
- 4 (8mm) frosted pink rondelle beads
- 5 (6mm) frosted pink round beads
- 2 (20mm) acrylic jewels or shank buttons with rhinestones
- 2 (16-inch) pieces of hot pink ⅞-inch-wide grosgrain ribbon
- 3 (14-inch) pieces of .7mm clear elastic cord
- 2 (¾ x ¼-inch) silver ribbon ends
- 2 (4–6mm) silver jump rings
- Household tape
- Scissors
- Chain- or needle-nose pliers with no teeth
- Big-eye needle
- Jewelry glue

3. Repeat step 2 with the next two elastic cords following patterns for strand 2 and strand 3 or using your own pattern. Apply a drop of glue to each knot. Set aside to let glue dry.

4. Cut one end of each ribbon on the diagonal (Figure 3).

Figure 3

5. Fold the other end of ribbon in about ¼ inch and over again (Figure 4). Slide one ribbon end over fold, center it on the ribbon, then squeeze it closed with pliers. Make sure to squeeze on both sides of the ribbon end and not to smash the loop. You can also squeeze across the ends, if you like. Repeat this step on the second piece of ribbon (Figure 5).

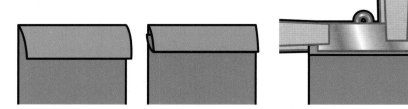

Figure 4   **Figure 5**

6. Trim the ends of elastic. Flip the top of your headband over so the bottoms of the jewels or buttons are faceup.

7. String one loop of a ribbon end and one loop of one acrylic jewel or the shank of a button onto an open jump ring. To open a jump ring, hold one side between your thumb and finger and the other side with the round-nose pliers. Make sure the opening is facing up. Gently twist the ends sideways to open. Do not pull the ends apart; this will break your jump ring (Figure 6). Twist the jump ring closed. Repeat this step with the other ribbon on the other end of the elastic band.

Figure 6

TO WEAR YOUR HEADBAND:

1. Pull your hair back into a bun or ponytail. Lay the elastic section around the bottom of your head and pull the ribbons up to the top. Tie a tight but comfortable knot. Take your headband off (Figure 7).

Figure 7   **Figure 8**

2. Put your headband over your head like a necklace with the elastic section in the front. Let down your hair and brush it into place. Gently pull your headband to the top of your head. Pull out your ears, if you like (Figure 8). ●

Lesson 9
Flower Power Earrings

Design by **Sharon Frank**

Make these earrings in bright and fun colors. You can mix and match them with your favorite outfits for a new look each day.

MAKE YOUR EARRINGS:

1. String beads on a head pin in this order: green E bead, yellow E bead, green flower focal bead, yellow E bead, green E bead (Figure 1).

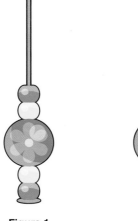
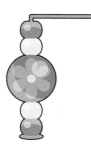

Figure 1   **Figure 2**

2. Push beads down to bottom of the head pin and place your thumbnail on top bead on head pin. Bend the head pin over to form an upside-down L shape. Measure about ⅜ inch from the bend and put a mark with a black marker. Use your side-cutting pliers to cut the pin at the mark (Figure 2).

t!p

Don't worry if your first loop isn't perfect. You can unroll the loop and try again. If the wire gets too many kinks in it, use your side-cutting pliers to trim the wire right above the beads and remove them. Start over with another head pin. Keep practicing and soon you will learn to make a great loop!

3. To create the simple loop, hold the earring with the tail away from you. Grasp end of the head pin in your round-nose pliers, about half way up the nose of the pliers. Roll the pliers toward you to create the loop. Keep rolling until the wire touches itself. You can stop part way through to adjust your pliers and complete the roll (Figure 3).

Figure 3

4. Adjust the loop with your pliers until it is in the center of your bead. It should look like a lollipop from the side (Figure 4).

Figure 4

5. To attach the beads to the fishhook earring finding, use your pliers to gently twist the loop opening to the side just far enough to slip over the loop of the earring finding (Figure 5).

Figure 5   **Figure 6**

6. Use your pliers to close the loop securely so it won't slide off the earring finding (Figure 6).

7. Repeat steps 1–6 to complete your second earring. ●

t!p

If you have one large bead in a design, it's called a focal bead. To keep the focus on that special bead, select beads for the remainder of your design that are smaller and less decorative. This will allow your focal bead to shine in your design.

Any style 10mm round bead will work in this design. Try your favorite 10mm round bead for this design to make it your own!

Lesson 10
Glitter Glam

Design by **Sharon Frank**

Glitter adds a little sparkle to these dangle earrings.

MAKE YOUR EARRING:

1. String E beads on the head pins in this order. Head pin 1: purple, green, pink. Head pin 2: green, purple, pink. Head pin 3: pink, green, purple (Figure 1).

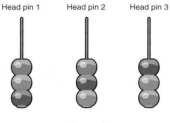

Head pin 1   Head pin 2   Head pin 3

Figure 1

2. On one beaded head pin, push beads down to the bottom of the head pin and place your thumbnail on the top bead on head pin. Bend the head pin over to form an upside-down L shape. Measure about ⅜ inch from the bend and put a mark with a black marker. Use your side-cutting pliers to cut the pin at the mark (Figure 2).

Figure 2   **Figure 3**

3. To create the simple loop, hold the earring with the tail facing away from you. Grasp end of the head pin in your round-nose pliers, about half way up the nose of the pliers. Roll the pliers toward you to create the loop. Keep rolling until the wire touches itself. You can stop part way through to adjust your pliers and complete the roll (Figure 3).

YOU WILL NEED:
- E beads: 6 purple, 6 pink, 6 green
- 2 (14mm) flower dangles
- 2 (5-link) lengths of silver cable chain
- 6 (1-inch) silver head pins
- 2 (6mm) silver jump rings
- 2 silver fishhook earring findings
- Round-nose pliers
- Chain-nose pliers
- Side-cutting pliers
- Ruler
- Black marker

4. Adjust the loop with your pliers until it is in the center of your bead. It should look like a lollipop from the side (Figure 4). Repeat steps 2–4 for remaining two head pins. Set these aside.

Figure 4

5. To open a jump ring, hold one side between your thumb and finger and the other side with the chain-nose pliers. Make sure the opening is facing up. Gently twist the ends sideways to open. Do not pull the ends apart; this will break your jump ring (Figure 5).

Figure 5

6. String the flower dangle onto the jump ring. String one end of a 5-link length of chain onto the jump ring. Close the jump ring by gently twisting the two ends back together so they fit tightly. Set aside (Figure 6).

Figure 6

t!p

Selecting beads with different finishes adds dimension to your jewelry. Try mixing glittered and non-glittered beads, glossy and satin-finished beads. We found our floral dangles in a package of flip-flop embellishments.

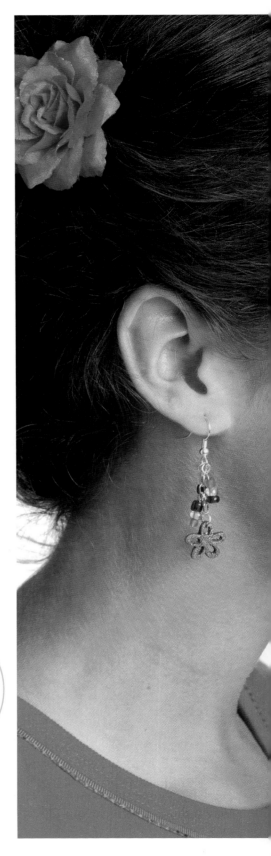

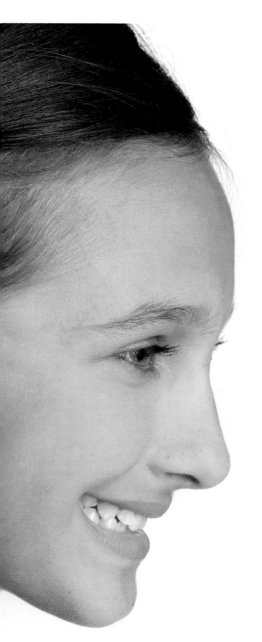

7. Hold the fishhook earring finding between your thumb and finger. With the chain-nose pliers, gently twist open the bottom ring on the earring finding. String the following onto the open ring: a beaded head pin, chain with flower dangle on it and a beaded head pin. Close the ring by gently twisting the ring back to its closed position (Figure 7).

Figure 7

8. Open the loop on the third beaded head pin using the same twisting motion you used to open the loop on the bottom of the fishhook finding. String the open loop onto the second chain link down from the top. Close the loop (Figure 8).

Figure 8

9. Repeat steps 1–8 to complete your second earring. ●

Lesson 11
Cherry Blast

Design by **Sharon Frank**

YOU WILL NEED:
- 20 pink E beads
- 22 (6mm) silver jump rings
- 2 silver fishhook earring wires
- Chain-nose pliers

Create this cute cluster of beads in your favorite color!

MAKE YOUR EARRING:

1. Open 10 jump rings. To open a jump ring, hold one side between your thumb and finger and the other side with the chain-nose pliers. Make sure the opening is facing up. Gently twist the ends sideways to open. Do not pull the ends apart; this will break your jump ring.

2. String one E bead on each jump ring. Close the jump rings by gently twisting the two ends back together so they fit tightly (Figure 1).

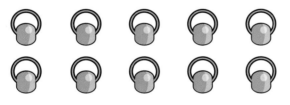

Figure 1

3. Open another jump ring referring to instructions in step 1. String on eight of the jump rings with E beads. Close the jump ring referring to instructions in step 2. Set aside (Figure 2).

Figure 2

Figure 3

4. Hold the fishhook earring finding between your thumb and finger. With the chain-nose pliers, gently twist open the bottom ring on the finding. String on one jump ring with E bead, the jump ring from step 3 and another jump ring with E bead. Close the loop (Figure 3).

5. Repeat steps 1–4 to complete your second earring. ●

t!p

Jump rings can be used for more than hooking pieces of your jewelry together. Combine them with small beads and they become a unique and fun design. Experiment with different ideas and see what you can design.